South West Coast

NATIONAL TR/

WALKS ALONG THE
SOUTH WEST COAST PATH

Ruth Luckhurst

PENZANCE TO ST IVES

A Coastal Publishing Limited Book

Editor Alison Moss
Design Jonathan Lewis
Production Peter Sills
South West Coast Path Project Manager Jo Kiddell

First published in 2013 by Coastal Publishing Limited
The Studio
Puddletown Road
Wareham
Dorset BH20 6AE

T: 01929 554195
E: enquiries@coastalpublishing.co.uk
www.coastalpublishing.co.uk

ISBN 978-1-907701-06-1

British Library Cataloguing-in-Publication Data
A catalogue record for this book is available from the British Library.

With great thanks to the South West Coast Path Team's partners, who help to maintain and
manage the Coast Path, for providing pictures and contributing to the research for this book.
In particular, we'd like to thank the Cornwall Area of Outstanding Natural Beauty (AONB),
the National Trust and Natural England, as well as all the wonderful photographers who have
supplied their pictures for use in this book.

South West Coast Path

NATIONAL TRAIL

The European Agricultural Fund for Rural Development: Europe investing in rural areas

Image Acknowledgements
(key: t:top, m:middle, b:bottom, l:left, r:right, c:centre)
Images in this book are copyright of the photographers and artists.

All Aerial photographs © Coastal Publishing Limited; Front cover
Dean Feast; Rod Allday 45m; Gillian Booth 15m; Ray Dot Culmer
8t; Ted Forman 4m, 63b; Jaap Gaasenbeek 62t; Terry Hawkes 14b;
Jason Holders 37t; Mike Hutchinson 58t; Grzegorz Jeneralek 29b;
Lalouette Photographers 9b; Katy Lawry 58m, 62b; Graham P Leese
5b; Ruth Luckhurst 14t, 15t, 22t, 23t, 23m, 23b, 33t, 33b, 36b,
40m, 41b, 44t, 48m, 54t, 54m, 55; Mike Mayor 8m, 40t; Colin
Milner 45t; Krzysztof Nowakowski 28t; David Peake 22b; Jennifer
Rowlandson 32b; Ian Scholey - www.newfolio.co.uk 33m; Jon
Speed 29t; Andrew Trenoweth 48t; Edward Webb 59.

CONTENTS

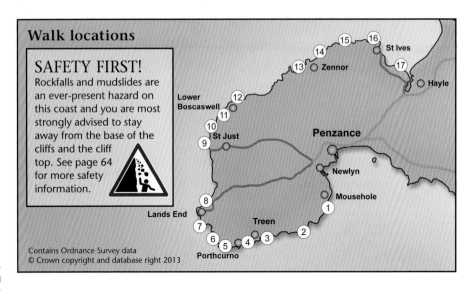

Walk locations

SAFETY FIRST!
Rockfalls and mudslides are an ever-present hazard on this coast and you are most strongly advised to stay away from the base of the cliffs and the cliff top. See page 64 for more safety information.

St Ives
15
16
14
13 Zennor
17
Hayle
Lower Boscaswell
12
11
10
9 St Just
Penzance
Newlyn
Mousehole
1
8
Lands End
7
Treen
6 5 4 3 2
Porthcurno

Contains Ordnance Survey data
© Crown copyright and database right 2013

West Penwith, from Penzance to St Ives, is a remote and rugged peninsula, a mysterious place of moor and heath, where buzzards wheel and peregrines dive, where ravens and jackdaws croak in the stunted bushes and swallows swoop along green lanes linked by granite stiles to ancient pathways through a patchwork field system dating back 5,000 years. Great lumps of granite rear from the bracken and heather, among ancient weathered monuments, and linnets and stonechats, warblers and wheatears, sing from the scrub of gorse and thorn.

At Lamorna, famous for the granite quarries that supplied the stone for the Thames Embankment and London buildings such as Lloyds Bank and New Scotland Yard, artist Samuel John 'Lamorna' Birch made his home. He was an active member of the Newlyn School of Painters, a group of artists drawn to this coast by the pure, clean air and the warmth. A tranquil haven, so it seems.

But appearances can be deceptive, as the old Penlee lifeboat house testifies, now serving as a memorial to the crew lost at sea

Gurnard's Head.

in the Penlee Lifeboat Disaster (see Walk 1). Lighthouses have been placed at strategic places to warn sailors of hidden rocks, as well as buoys with chiming bells and wailing whistles, and in the tiny coves the fishing boats are pulled up high on cobbled granite quays, out of the reach of powerful waves.

Porthcurno became the hub of British communications for many years when the first undersea cables were laid to link Britain to the rest of her Empire. Meanwhile, the cove's romantic aspects made it the perfect setting for one woman's dream of a Greek amphitheatre, a place where players could strut and fret their hour upon the open-air stage against a backdrop of stunning scenery.

INTRODUCTION

Land's End is bound up in romantic tales, from the lost land of Atlantis to the mythical drowned world of Lyonesse, which can be linked to the Scilly Isles when rising sea levels after the last Ice Age submerged parts of the landscape.

Legend aside, the landscape is overlain with many layers of history, going right back to the Stone Age. The 'quoits', or giant dolmens, where the Neolithic people buried their dead, are thought to have been used for the mystical rites of their ancestral cults, and the numerous stone circles, holed stones and menhirs probably played their part in these rituals. Defensive enclosures were constructed around settlements and the natural defences of cliffs were incorporated into promontory forts, while elsewhere, courtyard houses were built with the enigmatic underground 'fogou', only found in West Cornwall.

It was once an area of great mineral wealth, and tin and copper were worked here as long ago as the Bronze Age. The mining industry reached its zenith in the eighteenth and nineteenth centuries, when Cornwall led the way in the world's copper production and its miners and engineers were internationally renowned for their skills. There were hundreds of mines on the peninsula, with engine houses and chimney stacks above ground and a network of shafts leading deep beneath the sea.

This success led to its undoing as copper and tin prices collapsed when mining went global and one by one the mines closed. The engine houses and chimney stacks that remain stand as proud relics of its industrial past. In recognition of Cornish mining's role in the development of global mining, the area was designated a UNESCO World Heritage Site in 2006. www.cornishmining.org.uk

There is something for everybody in these walks, from strenuous hikes over the most rugged and remote parts to gentle strolls around the beaches and galleries of St Ives. Whether you want Celtic saints or medieval chapels, rare birds or basking sharks, mining museums or geological sites, Cornish pasties or dinosaur eggs, you will not be disappointed.

Public Transport

Most walks give information about the nearest car park. Information about public transport services for these walks can be found online at www.southwestcoastpath.com.

The Traveline South West website provides up-to-date information about all public transport links.
Visit www.travelinesw.com or call 0871 200 22 33.

INTRODUCTION

Cape Cornwall.

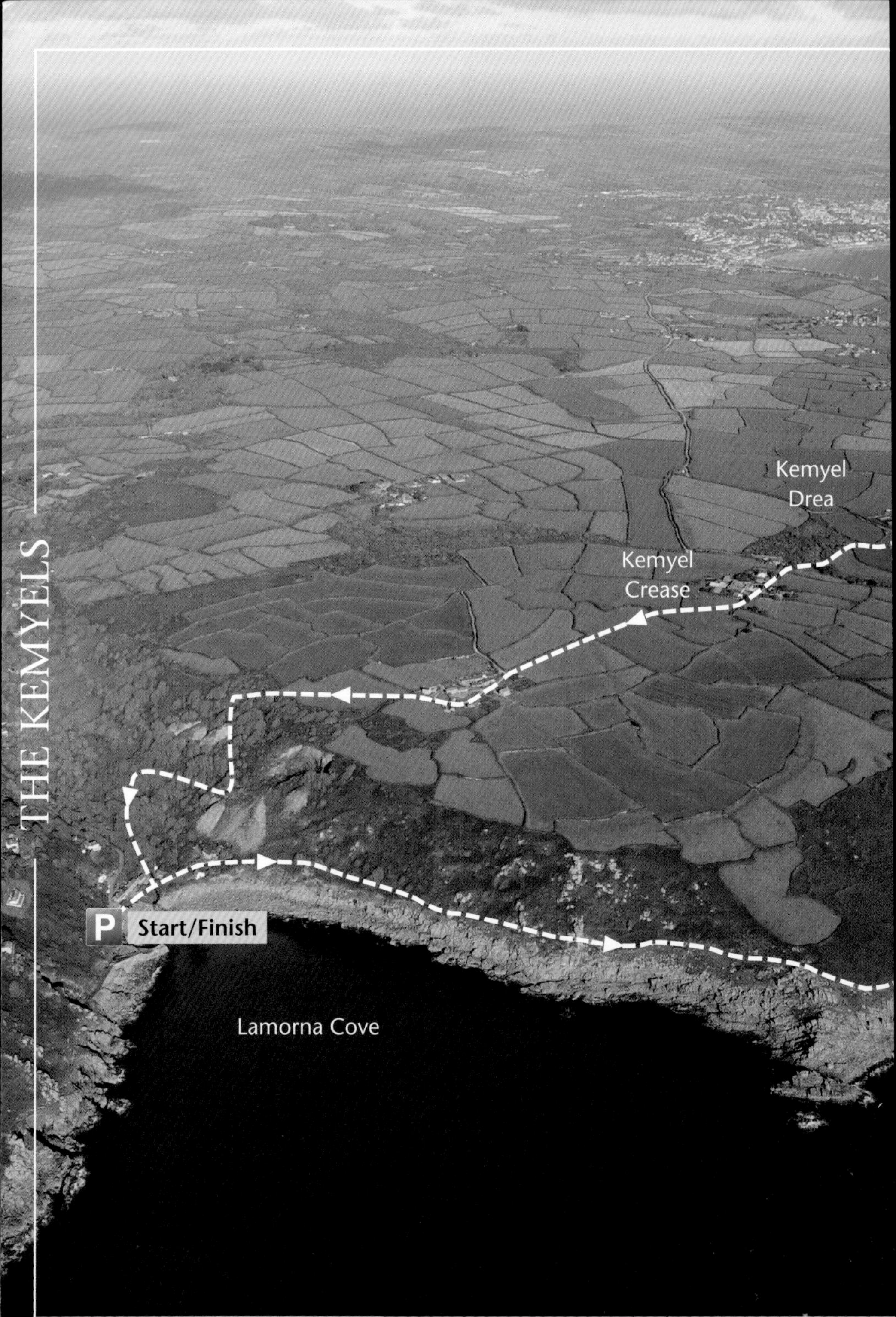

THE KEMYELS

Kemyel Drea

Kemyel Crease

P Start/Finish

Lamorna Cove

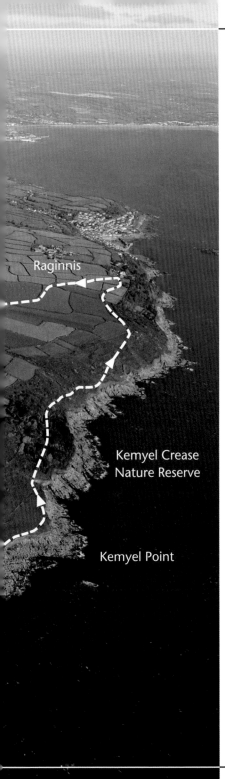

Raginnis

Kemyel Crease
Nature Reserve

Kemyel Point

Walk 1 – The Kemyels

Distance	3.75 miles (6km)
Estimated time	2 hours
Difficulty	● ● ○ ○ ○
Ascent	479ft (146m)
Map	OS Explorer Map 102
Starting point	SW 450240

Notes: A fairly easy walk through the pines and cypresses of the Kemyel Crease Nature Reserve, where Victorian gardeners once grew potatoes and daffodils in a patchwork of allotments. In places there is some stooping to clear the branches, and the walk returns inland through fields that may be muddy, so good footwear is recommended. There are short stretches of ascent and descent, but none of it is too strenuous.

From the Lamorna car park entrance, with your back to the sea, take the road to your right in front of the houses and pick up the South West Coast Path. Follow it around Kemyel Point, crossing the open ground beyond to go through the shrubs and trees of the Kemyel Crease Nature Reserve. Continue to Coastpath Cottage, just before Raginnis.

At the cottage take the footpath into the field to the left and follow it back above the Coast Path, through fields, to the farm at Kemyel Drea. Carry on past the farm buildings, through more fields to the road at Kemyel Crease. Turn left and walk past the buildings to take the footpath on the right beyond.

At Burnt Toast Cottage pick up the footpath to the front of the house and follow it through woods full of wildflowers, especially in the springtime, back to Lamorna Cove.

WALK 1

Lamorna Cove.

The South West Coast Path travels directly through the Kemyel Crease Nature Reserve, dividing it in two and leading walkers into a dappled green world as they make their way beneath the low canopy of branches. Although not a native species, Monterey pine was planted to provide shelter on this exposed part of the coast, because of its rapid growth and salt tolerance. Another fast-growing evergreen, Monterey cypress, was also introduced as a windbreak.

Fuchsia hedges were added in the late nineteenth century to mark out small flower and potato gardens, which could flourish in the south-facing, well-drained cliffs. At one time there were over a hundred of these gardens, or 'quillets' as they were known, and donkeys were used to work the land and carry seaweed up from the shore to use as a fertiliser. Flowers and potatoes ripened here much earlier in the season than anywhere else in Britain, thanks to the climate, and were taken by

Kemyel Crease Nature Reserve.

train to market in London. The gardens were being cultivated up until the 1930s.

The Kemyel Crease Nature Reserve is owned and managed by the Cornwall Wildlife Trust, who bought it in 1974.

In 1595, during the Anglo–Spanish War, Carlos de Amésquita landed with 400 men at Point Spaniard. The English militias, posted here to resist their advance, outnumbered the Spanish, but despite that they turned tail and fled, leaving just

12 men, under the leadership of Francis Godolphin, the Deputy Lord Lieutenant of Cornwall. In the ensuing hostilities, Penzance was bombarded by the Spanish fleet. Three ships were sunk and 400 houses destroyed. The settlements at Newlyn, Mousehole and Paul were burnt down, and in a final gesture of defiance the Spanish seized the cannon from the forts erected by Henry VIII along the coastline, put there specifically to repel the French and Spanish, and mounted them on their own ships.

Lamorna Cove was popular with members of the Newlyn School, a colony of artists drawn to the area by the unique quality of its light, its picturesque surroundings, and the warm climate which made it possible to paint out of doors for much of the year. Artists of the Newlyn School included Samuel John 'Lamorna' Birch, who arrived here from Lancashire in 1889, attracted by the presence of such eminent painters as Stanhope Forbes and his wife Elizabeth, who together founded the School of Painting in Newlyn in 1899. Samuel Birch added the 'Lamorna' to his name to distinguish himself from another local artist who shared his surname, and he lived in the old harbour-master's cottage at the top of Cove Hill.

The Penlee Lifeboat Disaster

The Union Star, a cargo-carrying coaster with eight people on board, got into difficulty on her maiden voyage between Holland and Ireland on 19 December 1981. Eight miles east of the Wolf Rock off St Mary's in the Scilly Isles, in winds gusting at speeds of up to 100 miles per hour, the ship reported engine failure. A Sea King helicopter was sent from RNAS Culdrose in an attempt to help, but it was unable to winch anyone to safety. Despite the appalling conditions, the Penlee Lifeboat at Mousehole, the Solomon Browne, was launched with a crew of eight men. As was the custom in operations that were particularly risky, just one crewmember per family was selected for the rescue.

After several attempts to get alongside the Union Star in 60-foot breakers, eventually the Solomon Browne was close enough for four people to board

it from the stricken coaster. However, before the rescue was complete both boats were lost with all hands.

When local lifeboat provision was later moved to Newlyn, the old Penlee lifeboat house was preserved as a memorial to those who died in the disaster, and the famous Mousehole Christmas lights are switched off for an hour each year on 19 December in remembrance of them.

Logan
Rock

Cribba
Head

Porthcurno

Finish

Porthguarnon

St Loy

Merthen Point

Boskenna
Cliff

Paynter's
Cove

Boscawen
Point

Zawn Gamper

Chough Zawn

Tater-du

Rosemodress
Cliff

Carn Barges

Tregurnow Cliff

Start

Lamorna
Cove

Walk 2 – Lamorna to Porthcurno

Distance	5.25 miles (8.5km)
Estimated time	2¾ hours
Difficulty	● ● ● ● ●
Ascent	1020 ft (311m)
Map	OS Explorer Map 102
Starting point	SW 450240

Notes: A strenuous hike high above white sandy coves and turquoise seas, and there are some sections of steep ascent and descent. Several buses run most days between Porthcurno and Lamorna (see page 5)

From the Lamorna car park walk to the end of the quay, on the western side of the cove, and take the South West Coast Path around Tregurnow Cliff, climbing Rosemodress Cliff and passing the lighthouse at Tater-du. Carry on towards Boscawen Point, passing above Zawn Gamper and Chough Zawn, bearing right to stay high as the path starts to round Boscawen Point and then dropping into the trees on Boskenna Cliff above Paynter's Cove and St Loy's Cove.

From here the path heads inland towards St Loy. Fork left at the top to continue through the trees and around Merthen Point and then climb high above Trevedran Cliff and Coffin Rock. At Porthguarnon the path drops steeply to the stream and ascends the other side, to pass Gazells and Le Scathe Cove. Fork left and left again to stay close to the cliffs as the path descends to Penberth.

On the far side of Penberth the path climbs steeply around Cribba Head and carries on around the back of Logan Rock and Treryn Dinas, passing above the sandy beaches to Porthcurno. Turn right to the car park.

WALK 2

Telegraph
Museum

Trendrennen

Treen

Porthcurno

P Start/Finish

Treryn Dinas

Logan Rock

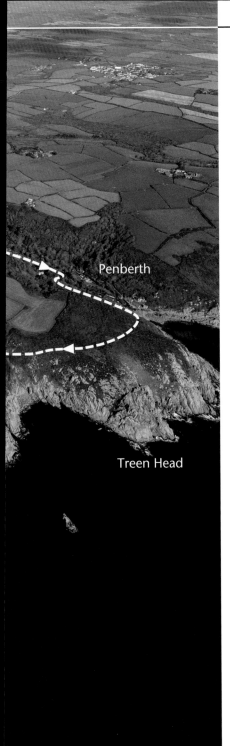

Penberth

Treen Head

Walk 3 – Porthcurno and Penberth

Distance	3.5 miles (5.5km)
Estimated time	1¾ hours
Difficulty	● ● ● ○ ○
Ascent	741ft (226m)
Map	OS Explorer Map 102
Starting point	SW 384223

Notes: A high coastal walk with breathtaking views, returning inland through Penberth, a village built of local granite and looking as though it is a natural part of the landscape. Take a short detour to view the precarious Logan Rock, and the spectacular prehistoric hillfort of Treryn Dinas at Treen Head. Although not a long walk, there are some steep gradients and the path is sometimes rocky.

From the main valley car park in Porthcurno, climb the steps at the back right-hand corner and turn left to follow the path along the access road past the Telegraph Museum. At the gate turn right and uphill, to bear left into a large field. Continue straight ahead, towards Trendrennen, through three fields to the right-hand end of the buildings.

Continue ahead on the track, past Trendrennen, turning right just after the second gate to walk across the field diagonally left. Carry on over a series of stiles, entering Treen on a track and forking right to the village car park. Take the footpath running left beyond the car park through fields to Penberth, following it down the valley to the cove. Cross the stream on the stone bridge, to take the South West Coast Path steeply uphill to the top and on to a junction of paths inland of Treen Head. Here bear right then fork left to continue along the cliff top.

WALK 3

When the path forks take either route, since the two run parallel and meet again at a junction of paths. Continue on the Coast Path, forking right along the hedged path. At the National Trust Porthcurno sign leave the main path to go left, descending steeply into Porthcurno; or for a less taxing descent, continue ahead at the National Trust sign.

Penberth Boats.

The tiny hamlet of Penberth was once a flourishing fishing village with a fleet of about 15 fishing boats, and although only a few boats still fish from here for local markets, it remains a working cove. Nowadays an electric winch is used to draw the boats up the granite slipway, but the massive man-powered capstan that once performed the task still has pride of place above the water. This was restored by the National Trust, who have owned Penberth since 1957, when it was transferred through the National Heritage Fund, in memory of those who died in the Second World War.

On the towering rocky promontory at Treryn Dinas ('Treen Castle') flint tools have been found dating back to the Mesolithic, or Middle Stone Age, and a Neolithic stone circle was recorded here by the local eighteenth-century antiquarian William Borlase (see Walk 12), although there is nothing to be seen of it now.

The ramparts and ditches of the Iron Age promontory fort are visible, however, defending the landward part of the headland, and the remains of stone houses inside the fort. Archaeologists have also found coins and a Roman copper brooch.

At the point of Treryn Dinas is the famous Logan Rock, or rocking stone. Pronounced 'loggan', the name is derived from an English dialect word meaning 'to rock', possibly from a Norse word for 'wagging the tail'. Despite weighing about 80 tons, the Logan Rock was dislodged in 1824 by

Logan Rock, Porthcurno.

a group of sailors led by Lieutenant Hugh Goldsmith, nephew of the writer Oliver Goldsmith.

The rock had become a popular tourist attraction, however, and the Admiralty was prevailed upon to restore the feature to its original position, with the help of 60 men using 13 capstans with blocks and chains from the dockyard at Plymouth, at a cost of £130 8s 6d.

Treryn Dinas.

Porthcurno was the termination of the first submarine cables laid between Britain and her empire. The first cable, to India via Carcavelos in Portugal in 1870, was followed by links to locations all over the globe. The quiet cove at Porthcurno was chosen, rather than a harbour such as Penzance or Falmouth, to reduce the chance of the cables being snagged or damaged by ships' anchors. Porthcurno became the hub of international cable communications for the next 100 years and remained the largest cable station in the world. Run initially by the Eastern Telegraph Company, later it merged with Marconi's Wireless Telegraph Company, founded by Guglielmo Marconi in 1897, four years before he sent the first radio signal across the Atlantic from Poldhu on the Lizard.

The Minack Theatre.

During the Second World War, the cable operations buildings at Porthcurno were vulnerable to attack, and Cornish miners were drafted in to dig secret bomb- and gas-proof tunnels through the granite to house an underground building and run the 14 cables securely out to sea.

'Minack' in Cornish means a rocky place, and the unique Minack Theatre has the Logan Rock headland as a stunning backdrop. During the summer months it stages a range of plays, from Shakespeare to contemporary works. The open-air theatre was the brainchild of Rowena Cade, daughter of the owner of a Derbyshire cotton mill and great-great-granddaughter of Joseph Wright, the 'painter of the industrial revolution'. Doing much of the heavy construction work herself, Cade brought to life a British version of an ancient Greek or Roman cliff theatre, and it opened in 1932 with a performance of The Tempest. Past performers here include Michael York, Sheridan Morley, John Nettles and Su Pollard.

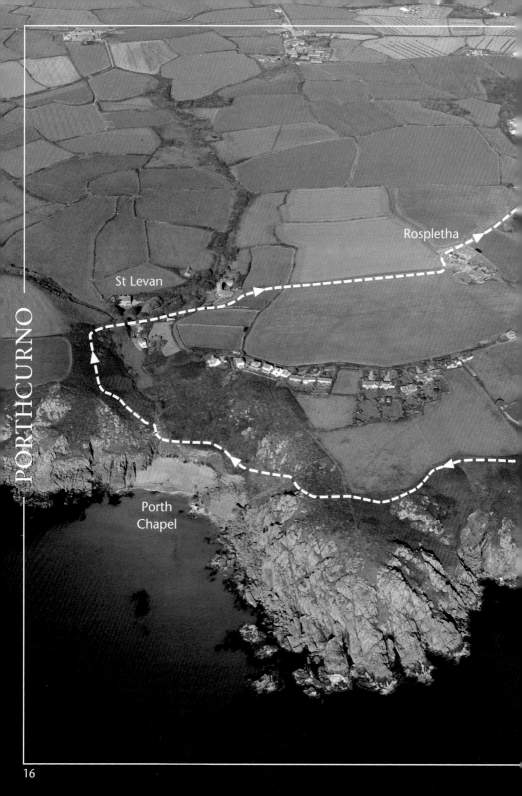

PORTHCURNO

Rospletha

St Levan

Porth
Chapel

Porthcurno

P Start/Finish

Minack
Theatre

Walk 4 – Porthcurno

Distance	1.5 miles (2.5km)
Estimated time	1 hour
Difficulty	● ○ ○ ○ ○
Ascent	259ft (79m)
Map	OS Explorer Map 102
Starting point	SW 384223

Notes: A small but inspiring coastal loop from Porthcurno around the headland at Pedn-Mên-an-Mere (Rocky Headland by the Sea), with great sea views, returning via St Levan and the church dedicated to the sixth-century saint on the hill above the remains of his ancient chapel and his holy well. Although there is some ascent and descent en route this is an easy walk taking in a small sandy beach that is perfect for a picnic.

From Porthcurno valley car park head down towards the beach, turning right at the granite marker post towards Porthgwarra. Climbing steadily, take the lower path to the Minack Theatre. Cross the car park to the kissing gate and follow the South West Coast Path past Rôspletha Cliffs (with an optional detour along the headland) to the beach at Porth Chapel, ignoring the paths inland to your right before you descend to the beach.

Follow the path climbing inland above the beach, passing St Levan's Well and branching right, until it comes to the road. Take the path from the churchyard back to Porthcurno, carrying straight on ahead along the bridleway at Rospletha. Turn right on the road at Porthcurno to return to the car park at the start of the walk.

WALK 4

Porth Loe

Coastwatch
Station

Gwennap Head
(Tol-Pedn-Penwith)

Porthgwarra

P

Start/Finish

Walk 5   Porthgwarra

Distance	1.25 miles (2km)
Estimated time	2½ hours
Difficulty	● ● ● ● ●
Ascent	118ft (36m)
Map	OS Explorer Map 102
Starting point	SW 370217

Notes: A small walk with enormous views. This is a very spectacular section of coast and there is plenty to see. The heathland and valley at Porthgwarra are very popular with birdwatchers, and in summer skylarks, stonechats, linnets and wheatears are commonly seen, with rare migrants often putting in an appearance too. The headland is also a great spot for seeing dolphins, and basking sharks are frequent summer visitors.

From the car park at Porthgwarra turn back onto the road and walk a short distance left to pick up the South West Coast Path, following it around Gwennap Head. Known locally as Tol-Pedn-Penwith ('the holed headland of Penwith'), its granite cliffs are seamed with chasms and caves, making it a very popular venue for rock-climbing. It is also renowned for its passing marine bird species such as Manx and Sooty's Shearwaters, skuas, petrels and whimbrels.

Turn right to pass the Coastwatch Station halfway around for a short walk, or continue to the beach below at Porth Loe, turning right onto the path beyond, heading back to Porthgwarra. The heathland between Porthgwarra and Land's End is almost completely open access and crossed by numerous small paths, so have a wander, navigating by the sea but keeping clear of the cliff-edge, which is crumbling in places. If the weather is fine, bring a picnic.

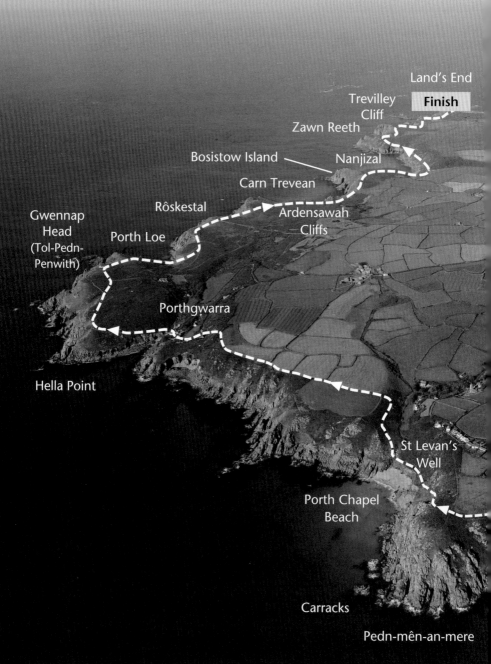

PORTHCURNO TO LAND'S END

Land's End

Finish

Trevilley
Cliff

Zawn Reeth

Bosistow Island

Nanjizal

Carn Trevean

Rôskestal

Ardensawah
Cliffs

Gwennap
Head
(Tol-Pedn-
Penwith)

Porth Loe

Porthgwarra

Hella Point

St Levan's
Well

Porth Chapel
Beach

Carracks

Pedn-mên-an-mere

Start

Porthcurno

Minack
Theatre

Walk 6 – Porthcurno to Land's End

Distance	5.25 miles (8.5km
Estimated time	2¾ hours
Difficulty	● ● ● ● ●
Ascent	751ft (229m)
Map	OS Explorer Map 102
Starting point	SW 384223

Notes: A strenuous but rewarding high-level walk through a rugged granite boulder field, catching the bus back to Porthcurno. Look out for butterflies and yellow-ringed dragonflies in the profusion of wildflowers in the summer. Keep clear of the cliff edge, which is crumbling in places.

From the car park in Porthcurno take the road down to the beach, turning right to pick up the South West Coast Path towards Porthgwarra and taking the lower path through the Minack Theatre car park to walk around Pedn-mên-an-mere and Carracks. The path then drops towards Porth Chapel Beach, pulling up past St Levan's Well.

Fork left above Porth Chapel to carry on along the Coast Path to Porthgwarra. The Coast Path carries on above the beach to climb Hella Point and Gwennap Head. Continue past Porth Loe and around Rôskestal and Ardensawah Cliffs.

Continue past the outcrop of Carn Trevean to the promontory fort at Bosistow Island, descending to the beach at Nanjizal. Cross the stream on the footbridge. After Carn Cravah the path drops to the little cove at Zawn Reeth and then climbs Trevilley Cliff, the first of a series of small headlands between here and Land's End, running between a number of carns (crags) and zawns (gullies) to reach Land's End.

St Levan was a sixth-century Celtic saint, born near St Buryan, who established a hermitage near the beach at Porth Chapel, linked by about 50 stone steps to his holy well and baptistry on the hillside above. The name is a corruption of St Selevan, the Celtic form of Solomon.

Porthgwarra Beach Tunnel.

On the south side of the Parish Church is the St Levan Stone, considered in pagan times to be a source of mystical power, especially in fertility rites. It is split cleanly into two halves, said to be a result of St Levan striking the rock with his staff after resting on it following a day's fishing. According to legend, when a packhorse with panniers can ride between the two halves, then the world will end.

A tall cross beside the stone is said to have been erected to sanctify the pagan site. In addition, there were at least five more Celtic crosses in the outlying district, marking the various paths to the church. One remains at the northeast corner of the churchyard, and another on the footpath towards Rospletha.

The tiny secluded cove at Porthgwarra is one of Britain's best birdwatching sites. The frequent sightings of rare species have included Yellow-browed Warbler, Dusky Warblers and Red-eyed Vireo.

Soft-plumaged Petrel and Black-browed Albatross have also been sighted at nearby Gwennap Head.

Miners from St Just apparently excavated the tunnel from the slipway towards the road at Porthgwarra to enable farmers to gather seaweed for fertilising the fields. There is a second tunnel, leading seawards, which gave access to the tidal 'hulleys' built in the rocks to store shellfish.

About a mile off Gwenapp Head lies the Runnel Stone, a hazardous rock pinnacle which used to be visible to passing vessels at low water until a steamship struck it in 1923. There is a buoy marking its position, fitted with a flashing light, a bell which peals with the movement of the waves, and a whistle set in a tube, whose

Nanjizal.

mournful noise can be heard clearly from Gwennap Head when there is a heavy swell. There are also two markers on the Head to warn sailors of the rock's position, and the former coastguard building is now a Coastwatch station.

Around Land's End archaeologists have found and been able to date a number of ancient artefacts. These include flint tools from the Middle and Late Stone Ages, as well as a cup-marked stone and a socketed stone, both from the Iron Age. There are also traces of Bronze and Iron Age middens, an Iron Age courtyard house and a Romano–British Round (an enclosed settlement dating from between 800 BC and AD 409).

Porth Chapel Beach and St Levans Well.

The granite around Land's End was formed some 275 million years ago. If you look closely at the granite boulders you pass, you will see that they contain very large white feldspar crystals: a sign that the molten rock cooled down very slowly after it was forced through much the older rocks. The mineralisation of the rocks during this process is what made Cornwall such an important mining area. As well as the tin for which the county was renowned, and the copper which made it a world leader in the mineral industry during the eighteenth and nineteenth centuries, lead, zinc and silver were also mined in the county.

Slow cooling crystals in granite.

The classic castellated coastline, with its large rectangular blocks and long narrow buttresses making it the best and most spectacular of its type in Britain, is a result of the action of the sea on the hard granite. As the Atlantic hurls massive breakers at the cliffs, compressed air is forced into the lines of weakness in the rock, eventually creating new caves, fissures, blowholes and zawns (or gullies).

Porthgwarra.

WALK 6

Sennen
Cove

Pedn-mên-du

Maen
Castle

Castle
Zawn

Dr Syntax's
Head

Land's End

Dr Johnson's Head

Start/Finish

Walk 7 – Land's End

Distance	2.5 miles (4km)
Estimated time	1¼ hours
Difficulty	● ● ○ ○ ○
Ascent	433ft (132m)
Map	OS Explorer Map 102
Starting point	SW 345249

Notes: Land's End is England's most westerly point. In spring and summer it is a riot of colour, when the gorse and heather are in bloom, and the pink thrift and white sea campion grow in banks between them. Dolphins and basking sharks can be spotted offshore, and sometimes a chough, Cornwall's national bird.

From the far end of the Land's End car park take the path to the right in front of the buildings, between the "stone circle" and the children's playground, and follow it seawards to join the South West Coast Path at Dr Syntax's Head. Turn right to follow the Coast Path towards Pedn-mên-du (Black Stone Headland).

As you approach the headland you pass Maen Castle, one of the many Iron Age promontory forts defending the coastline some 2,000 years ago. In March 2003, the RMS Mulheim was wrecked in the bay below and broke in two before the swell drove it into the inlet at Castle Zawn, where the remains can still be seen from the cliff above.

Rounding Pedn-mên-du, continue ahead for a detour to Sennen Cove; but otherwise turn right on the road, taking the right-hand path at the junction beyond to walk around the edges of the fields above the Coast Path, turning right on the road at the end to return to the car park.

WALK 7

Sennen
Cove

Land's End

Carn Boel

Start/Finish P

Mayon

Nanjizal

Mayon
Farm

Bosistow

Nanjizal
House

Higher
Bosistow

Polgigga

Trengothal Farm

Trebehor

Walk 8 – Sennen Cove and Land's End

Distance	7.25 miles (11.67km)
Estimated time	3½ hours
Difficulty	• • • • •
Ascent	711ft (217m)
Map	OS Explorer Map 102
Starting point	SW 350263

Notes: A long and bracing walk across the farmland above Sennen Cove, returning around the rugged and romantic coastline from Nanjizal with its sandy beach and hidden caves. Pause here for a picnic, or stop for refreshments among the spectacular rocky views at Land's End on your way back.

From the harbour car park in Sennen Cove walk past the RNLI shop and turn right onto Stone Chair Lane, following it uphill to the road. Take the footpath opposite and walk through fields to Mayon, crossing the main road and carrying on along the footpath to the left of Mayon Farm. Walking straight ahead through the fields to the road, turn left and pick up the bridleway ahead as the road turns left. Continuing ahead on the lane, take the footpath right at Trengothal Farm across fields to Trebehor, continuing across the road and walking to the main road at Polgigga.

Turn left on the road and then right at the crossroads to Bosistow, turning left before the farm entrance and continuing to Higher Bosistow. At Nanjizal House bear right and then fork right, to take the bridleway past Nanjizal and onto the South West Coast Path.

A detour here takes you to the delightfully secluded beach at Nanjizal; but otherwise turn right and follow the Coast Path, past the

Land's End.

buildings at Land's End and the rocky headlands beyond, to return to the car park at Sennen Cove.

A little way beyond the Kettle's Bottom rocks, about a mile to the west of Land's End, are several islets known as The Longships. Most of them are submerged except at low tide, but the three largest – Tal-y-Maen, Carn Bras, and Meinek – remain above the high water mark at all tides. The Longships are a popular place for diving.

The division of ocean currents at Land's End makes the water especially turbulent during storms, an effect described by Victorian artist John Ruskin as 'an entire disorder of the surges'. Combined with the numerous submerged rocks and islets, this made Land's End a treacherous place for shipping, and in 1795 Trinity House had a lighthouse built on the largest Longship, Carn Bras, for which it paid an annual rent of £100. With Carn Bras at just 12 metres

above sea level, the base of the 24 metre tower was often underwater, however, and in the 1870s the current, much higher, tower was built.

Doctor Syntax's Head is a spectacular granite headland, named after a fictitious schoolmaster who appeared in art publisher Rudolph Ackerman's Poetical Magazine between 1809 and 1820. Variously entitled 'The Tour of Doctor Syntax In Search of the Picturesque/In Search of Consolation/ In Search of a Wife', this humorous series of adventures was written in verse by Dr William Combe and illustrated by the renowned caricaturist Thomas Rowlandson.

Doctor Samuel Johnson, commemorated in the headland to the west of Doctor Syntax's, wrote the first Cornish Declaration of Independence in 1755, asserting Cornwall's rights to self-government as granted to the ancient tinners' Stannary Parliament by Edward III when he created the Duchy of Cornwall in 1337.

The Lost Worlds of Atlantis and Lyonesse

Land's End is associated with the mythical Cornish land of Lyonesse, believed by some to be the fabled lost world of Atlantis. The Greek philosopher Plato was the first to mention Atlantis, which he described in the fourth century BC as being more than 9,000 years old, with walls of gold and silver. He located it off the Strait of Gibraltar, and declared that it had been laid waste by the gods after its people became wicked and corrupt.

In 1997 the Moscow Institute of Meta-History sent a team to investigate a hill on the Atlantic seabed, just 100 miles off Land's End, known as Little Sole Bank and considered by the Institute to correspond to Plato's siting of Atlantis. The hill is at the edge of the Celtic Shelf, which was above sea level until it was flooded at the end of the last Ice Age, 10,000 years ago.

The drowned world of Lyonesse is more widely believed to be associated with the Scilly Isles, some of which were one landmass as recently as Roman times. Like other parts of western Cornwall, the Scilly Isles have been inundated by rising sea levels within the last 5,000 years, and it has been suggested that the story of Lyonesse is a folk memory of the event.

In Mount's Bay there are petrified tree stumps from a submerged forest, and the remains of ancient stone walls, and there are many sites in West Penwith where evidence has been found of human settlements dating as far back as Mesolithic times (8000–3000 BC).

In his fifteenth-century Morte d'Arthur, Thomas Mallory named Lyonesse as the birthplace of the knight Tristan. Alfred Lord Tennyson elaborated on the idea in the Idylls of the King, his own nineteenth-century Arthurian romance, making Lyonesse the site of the last battle between Arthur and Mordred.

Land's End.

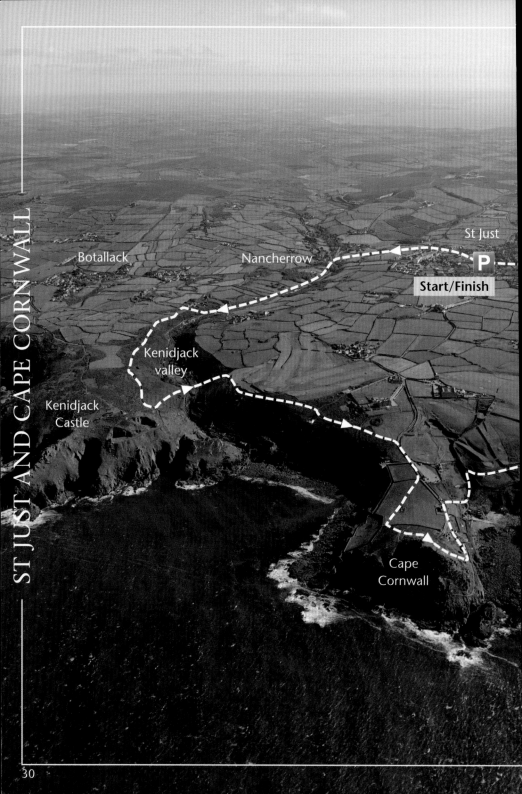

Botallack

Nancherrow

St Just

P

Start/Finish

Kenidjack
valley

Kenidjack
Castle

Cape
Cornwall

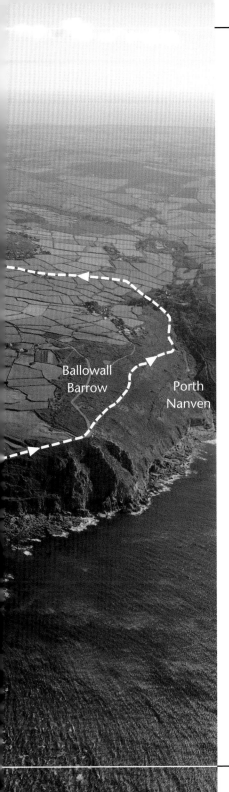

Ballowall
Barrow

Porth
Nanven

Walk 9 – St Just and Cape Cornwall

Distance	5.25 miles (6.75km)
Estimated time	2 hours
Difficulty	● ● ● ○ ○
Ascent	512ft (156m)
Map	OS Explorer Map 102
Starting point	SW 371314

Notes: A moderate walk through an area whose rich mineral reserves gave rise to a large and lively population over many centuries. Its archaeological treasures include industrial mills and mines, as well as ancient forts and settlements, and medieval churches and oratories, and Dinosaur Egg Beach is a protected site because of its geological importance. The paths are mostly good and the gradients are manageable.

From Market Square in St Just walk down Church Street, with the parish church on the left, to Venton Square East, bearing slightly left on the path. At the bottom turn left along the road and follow it round to the B3306 at Nancherrow. Cross this and go along the lane opposite, climbing the valley side and forking right and right again.

Bearing right on the track, turn left onto the the grassy lane and follow the South West Coast Path to the ruins of Kenidjack Castle. From the left of the building descend to a quarry track and turn left. Fork right to the valley bottom and take the next path on the right, crossing the footbridge to climb the other side and turn right at the top. Bear right at the junction and turn right immediately before the access road to Cape Cornwall.

Going into the field with the ruins of St Helen's Oratory, cross the stile at the far end onto the path. Turn left uphill at the outcrop to walk to

WALK 9

the top. Descend towards the car park, turning right down the track before it. At the bottom turn left, then go sharp right, still climbing. Go ahead on the lane then fork right opposite the trig point to follow the Coast Path along the cliff and down into the Cot Valley. Detour right to the tiny boulder-strewn beach at Porth Nanven, or turn left up the lane and climb steadily back to St Just, turning right at the top and then left, past the car park and toilets, to return to Market Square.

For many years Cape Cornwall was thought to be England's most westerly point, and it marks the point where the Atlantic waters divide, with some flowing north into the Bristol Channel and the Irish Sea, and some going into the English Channel. It is one of only two capes in Britain – a cape being a place where two bodies of water meet. The other is Cape Wrath, in the far northwest of Scotland, where the Atlantic meets the North Sea.

The landmark tower on the cape is the chimney stack of the former Cape Cornwall Mine, which worked to extract tin and copper from beneath the sea between 1836 and 1879.

Some 4,000 years ago there was a burial site here, and later, in the Iron Age, it was a promontory fort, or cliff castle. In the field below are the remains of St Helen's Oratory, an old chapel. Although the chapel is probably medieval, the site has been in use as a holy place since some time around the fourth century, and there was once an ancient cross with the chi rho christogram on it. The man who found it, a nineteenth-century vicar of St Just, took it back to the vicarage for safekeeping; but his successor is said to have thrown it down a well.

The Tregeseal river running through the Kenidjack or Nancherrow Valley just north of St Just was a valuable power source for the tin streams and other workings along the valley, and in the 1850s it was an uninterrupted mass of industry, with 50 working waterwheels, including the second biggest in the country. The pond in the valley bottom was once the reservoir for one of these wheels. Immediately to the left of the path early in the walk are the

Cape Cornwall.

conserved remains of the Carn Praunter Stamps, which operated for most of the nineteenth century, recently restored by the St Just Regeneration Project.

A track still runs alongside the stream, and downstream it runs into Porthledden Cove, a pebbly beach with excellent views and a good place for seal spotting. The river tumbles over rocky boulders into the sea, passing the substantial remains of the wheelpit which formerly housed the 32-foot waterwheel of Wheal Call or Boswedden Mine.

Carn Praunter Stamps.

Of the many burial monuments along this coastline, Ballowall Barrow is one of the most dramatic and complex. Lying on the hillside below the trig point at Carn Gloose ('grey rock' in Cornish), it dates back to the Bronze Age, and possibly earlier to the Late Stone Age. In the centre of the barrow were five cists, or stone-lined burial chambers, with a further two outside the stone platform and enclosing the central mound.

Porth Nanven sunset with The Brisons behind.

Porth Nanven is a place beloved of birdwatchers, who come here hoping to see a rarity such as the Yellow-billed Cuckoo, sighted in 1999. The mouth of the Cot Valley, with its lush sub-tropical vegetation and its many remnants of the old mining industry, is also known as Dinosaur Egg Beach and it is an important geological site. The large round boulders fell from the cliffs above and piled up on a wave-cut platform, created when the land was relieved of its weight of ice following the last Ice Age and the beach rose above sea level. It is illegal to remove these boulders. If you detour to look at the beach, watch out for rocks falling from the unstable and heavily mined cliffs.

Sennen Cove.

WALK 9

Pendeen

P Start/Finish

Geevor
Mine

Levant
Mine

The
Crowns

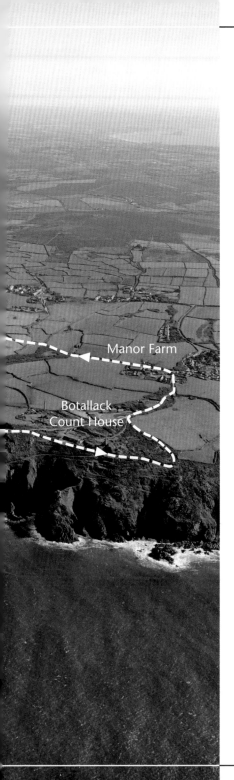

Manor Farm

Botallack
Count House

Walk 10 – Levant, Botallack and the Crowns

Distance	3 miles (4.75km)
Estimated time	1½ hours
Difficulty	•• • • •
Ascent	240ft (73m)
Map	OS Explorer Map 1021
Starting point	SW 383344

Notes: An easy walk through part of the Cornish Mining World Heritage Site, in a landscape divided into tiny fields by ancient stone walls and dotted with chimneys and engine houses, including the spectacular Crowns engine houses at Botallack Mine. Visit the Botallack Count House and the Levant Beam Engine, both restored and maintained by the National Trust.

From the car park at Pendeen, opposite the Boscaswell Stores, turn left and walk to the Geevor Tin Mine entrance, turning down the drive following the sign to Levant. Turn left just beyond the buildings, bearing right on the unsurfaced track and turning left at the boulder to head towards the tall chimney.

Coming to Levant Mine, follow the bottom edge of its car park and then pick up the South West Coast Path to the Botallack Count House. Turn left off the Coast Path and continue to Manor Farm and take the lane to the left beyond, following the footpath straight ahead through the tiny fields of Carnyorth Moor. On reaching the lane turn right, bearing left with it to arrive at Levant Road. Turn right and take the road almost opposite, turning right onto the footpath beyond the farm, returning through the fields to Geevor Mine. From here retrace your steps to the car park.

WALK 10

In 2006 the Cornish Mining World Heritage Site was created, in recognition of the important cultural contribution made globally by Cornish mining and miners. It comprises 10 areas, each of which retains authentic and historically significant aspects of the Cornwall and West Devon mining landscapes.

The St Just Mining District is especially noteworthy for the dramatic locations of some of its mines. There is a geological boundary here between the granite of Land's End and the 'killas' (the local name for Upper Devonian slate) north of Cape Cornwall. Here the almost vertical veins of tin and copper occur at right angles to the coast, and both Botallack and Levant Mines were sited on the very edge of the cliff to be closer to these lodes.

Tin, and probably copper, were being produced here 4,000 years ago, in the Bronze Age, and the tin streaming methods developed were used until the end of the medieval period, when shafts and tunnels had to be dug as the near-surface ore ran out. The rocks were initially broken manually, and then techniques including fire-setting were used before gunpowder was introduced to Cornwall for blasting, in 1689. For this, gunpowder was first packed into holes bored in the rock face and then fired to advance the levels or sink shafts. As the mines got deeper, so the miner's job became more difficult and more dangerous, and water became an increasing problem. Cornish engineers and inventors were, in time, to push the limits of what was possible with existing steam technology, placing them at the forefront of industrial development.

In the eighteenth century an increasing knowledge of the geological processes causing mineralisation led to a better idea of where ore bodies may be found. This development, together with the improved efficiencies of the steam engine led to a greater increase in productivity. As a result, Cornish mining had a tremendous impact on the industrialisation of Britain.

In the century between 1815 and 1915, when mineral production elsewhere in the world was to eventually cause a slump in copper and tin prices, between 250,000 and 500,000 Cornish migrated in search of work, taking with them tremendous skills in deep mining through hard rock. By the 1990s the era of Cornish mining had drawn to a close.

An audio trail for Botallack Count House is available from the Cornish WHS website.

Levant Beam Engine

The famous Levant Beam Engine is the only Cornish beam engine anywhere in the world that is still powered by steam on its original mine site. Housed in the engine house perched on the edge of the cliffs, it was restored after 60 years of disuse, by a group of dedicated volunteers known as the Greasy Gang.

The steam engine as used for pumping was originally developed by Dartmouth ironmonger and engineer Thomas Newcomen in 1712 as his Atmospheric Engine. The force from a vertically operating piston was applied to pump rods in a mine shaft via a connecting rod and pivoted overhead beam, or 'bob'. Scottish engineer James Watt improved on the design, patenting an engine using less than a third of the fuel while still doubling the output, and he and Matthew Boulton provided many of the engines powering

the mines towards the end of the eighteenth century.

In 1771 Richard Trevithick of Illogan, the other side of St Ives, was appointed engineer at Ding Dong Mine near Land's End, and here he devised a high-pressure steam engine that was more efficient again. Although Bolton and Watt went to Parliament in a vain attempt to make high-pressure steam engines illegal on safety grounds, following the expiry of their patent in 1800 Trevithick's Cornish Engine was widely adopted and adapted throughout the industry.

The Botallack Count House was built around 1861 to accommodate the Captain and staff of the Botallack Mine and provide their office space. Miners would be paid here, and shareholders would be treated to lavish dinners when they gathered to view the accounts.

GEEVOR AND CHÛN QUOIT

Chûn
Castle

Keigwin
farm

Morvah

Chypraze

Portheras Cove

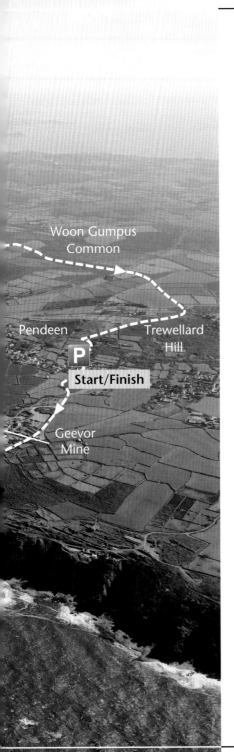

Woon Gumpus Common

Pendeen

Trewellard Hill

P

Start/Finish

Geevor Mine

Walk 11 – Geevor and Chûn Quoit

Distance	6.5 miles (10.5km)
Estimated time	3 hours
Difficulty	● ● ● ● ○
Ascent	735ft (224m)
Map	OS Explorer Map 102
Starting point	SW 383344

Notes: A long and fairly strenuous loop around the historic St Just Mining District, climbing to the moorland above, with its granite tors and its prehistoric settlements and ancient monuments. There are dramatic views over coast and countryside with optional guided tours round a tin mine and a lighthouse.

From the car park at Pendeen, opposite the Boscaswell Stores, turn left and go through the Geevor Tin Mine entrance to walk down the drive to the South West Coast Path. Turn right and walk across the footbridge a little further ahead, continuing over the hill to a stream valley. Reaching the road at the coastguard cottages turn left and walk towards the lighthouse, passing in front of it to head towards Portheras Cove, and following the Coast Path signs along the cliff above the beach.

Head inland across the stepping stones to climb out of the little valley, leaving the Coast Path at the sign to Morvah, instead carrying on uphill, past the farm at Chypraze, to follow the lane up to the B3306. Turn right and then sharp left at the gallery to walk along a sunken farm lane past the Keigwin farms. Turn right at the waymark to Chûn Castle, staying on the track as it turns right and ignoring two further paths right.

WALK 11

Chimneys and stuctures of Geevor and Levant mines.

Continue to Chûn Quoit – with an optional detour to Chûn Castle – and take the tiny path through the heather on the first right, aiming towards Carn Kenidjack. Cross the field ahead and follow the track from Woon Gumpus Common to the car park. Continue straight ahead on Trewellard Hill, taking the track to the right at Wheal Bal and crossing Trewellard Common, ignoring two turns to the right and continuing ahead, past the church and houses, to the road. Turn right to return to the Pendeen car park.

Kenidjack Holed Stone.

The area around Geevor was originally known as 'Stennack an Gever' (The Tin Stream of the Goat), and when the tin concentrate sent from here to be processed on Humberside was returned in ceremonial tin ingots, these were stamped with a fish-tailed goat to denote their origin.

By the eighteenth century there was a large number of underground mines

(or setts) working tin and copper on the Geevor site, although the discovery of new international copper reserves had a dramatic effect on the price of metal, and there was a corresponding slump in Cornish mining (see Walk 10). After this, many of Cornwall's miners took their extensive skills abroad in search of work, and by 1891 the North Levant Mine had stopped working.

In 1899, a group of St Just miners who had migrated to South Africa were forced by the Second Boer War to return home, and after a careful exploration of the area's remaining mineral reserves they set up the Levant North (Wheal Geevor) in 1901. In 1904 the Western Australian Gold Field Company bought into it and the Geevor Tin Mine Company was formed as a result, in 1911. Combining Geevor, North Levant and Wheal Carne and covering 208 acres, Geevor Tin Mine gradually expanded over the next 10 years, with large investments in facilities and equipment, to become one of the biggest tin mines in the country, and the largest employer in the district.

After the First World War a new shaft was sunk, called Victory Shaft, and over the next few decades this was extended to connect with shafts exploiting new lodes discovered throughout the district. With an important sub-incline shaft opening in 1980, plans were in place to sink a further sub-incline shaft connecting Geevor to the Botallack sett, refurbishing Allen's shaft near Botallack Count House and setting new headgear in place over it.

All this came to nothing, when the price of tin crashed, almost overnight, from over £10,000 a ton to £3,500 a ton. New reserves of alluvial tin had been discovered in Malaya and Brazil, and the USA released its strategic tin stockpile on the open market in London's Metal Exchange. It was the death knell for Cornish mining. Geevor struggled on for a few years, but it closed in 1990, the last working tin mine in West Penwith.

It has been preserved as the largest mining heritage site in the UK. The surface buildings still house the winders and compressors used in the mine after the introduction of electricity and compressed air, and there is a museum with a collection of artefacts, displays and photographs of minerals, mines and miners, as well as underground tours.

Carn Kenidjack (or Hooting Cairn) is a granite tor on the downs above Botallack. Nearby is the Tregeseal Stone Circle, also known as The Dancing Stones and The Nine Maidens. This was once part of a ritual complex of two or even three stone circles, thought to date back to the late Neolithic or early Bronze Age, with a number of associated holed stones in the surrounding heather and a large menhir some distance to the east. There is also a chambered cairn, the Tregeseal Barrow, where a Bronze Age urn containing cremated remains was found. This is now in the British Museum.

An audio trail for Geevor to Levant is available from the Cornish WHS website.

Carn Kenidjack Stone Circle.

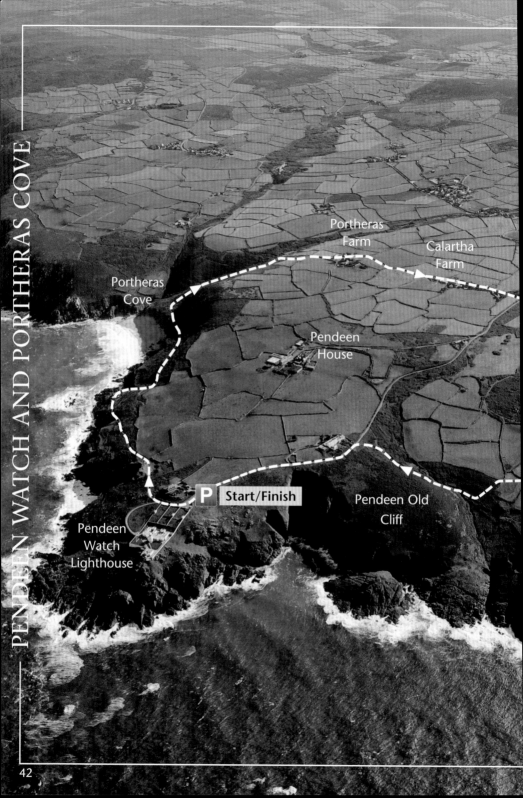

PENDEEN WATCH AND PORTHERAS COVE

Portheras Farm

Calartha Farm

Portheras Cove

Pendeen House

P Start/Finish

Pendeen Old Cliff

Pendeen Watch Lighthouse

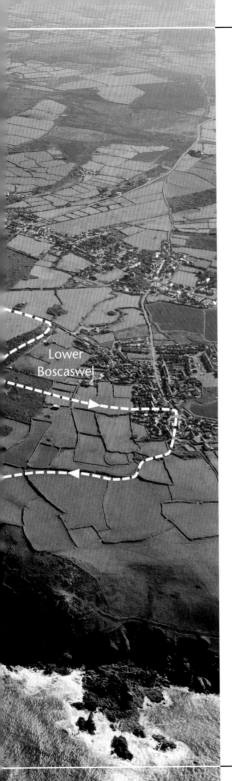

Lower
Boscaswel

Walk 12 – Pendeen Watch and Portheras Cove

Distance	4.25 miles (7km)
Estimated time	2½ hours
Difficulty	● ● ● ● ○
Ascent	803ft (245m))
Map	OS Explorer Map 111
Starting point	SW 379358

Notes: A short stroll through fields and heathland, with just gentle ascent and descent. There are great sea views and an optional lighthouse tour (during opening hours), as well as a tiny sandy beach at Portheras Cove. Like the rest of Penwith, this is an area that has been inhabited for many millennia, and Pendeen and Boscaswell are both famous for their 'fogou', or underground chambers.

Parking in the car park at Pendeen Watch Lighthouse, turn left onto the South West Coast Path and follow it above Pendeen Cliff, ignoring the first path to your right, unless you want a detour to Pendeen House (although this is not open to the public). Take the next path inland to the right, above Portheras Cove, (unless you wish to detour to the beach), continuing ahead up the hillside when a path joins from the left and following the path to the right at the end of the valley, to reach Portheras Farm.

Turn left briefly on the lane and take the footpath on the right, through fields to Calartha Farm. Following the path on the left-hand side of the buildings, fork right on the drive and take the lane straight ahead into Lower Boscaswell. Bearing right, walk through the village, bearing right towards the bottom of the village and then turning right to turn left onto the lane towards Pendeen Old Cliff, carrying on along the footpath

Pendeen Lighthouse.

beyond to rejoin the Coast Path. Follow the Coast Path back to the lighthouse.

The lighthouse at Pendeen Watch is the last shore station on West Cornwall's north coast before Land's End, and it is one of Trinity House's visitor centres, with tours of the machinery as well as the tower. Built at the turn of the nineteenth century, much of the rocky outcrop it stands on had to be removed to accommodate the squat white tower, as well as the keepers' cottages and the foghorn. The engine house is a listed building and is the only place in the country to have kept its 12-inch siren with the associated machinery.

Pendeen House was a good place to live for anyone fascinated by prehistory. Within its grounds there was the Pendeen vau, or fogou. From the Cornish word meaning 'cave', a fogou is an ancient underground chamber. At Pendeen this consists of three passages: a central one some 8 or 9 metres long, with two smaller ones branching from it at one end, and the sloping walls are covered by stone slabs. It dates from the Iron Age or the Romano–British period (800 BC – AD 409), and it was excavated in 1769 by William Borlase, who was born here (see opposite).

There is another fogou at Lower Boscaswell. Dating from the same period, it is somewhat smaller and in poor condition. It is enclosed within a thick drystone wall forming the west side of an oval enclosure, thought to be part of a courtyard house. A raised platform of earth and stone extending from it is likely to be another oval enclosure, also part of the courtyard complex. Roman coins and pottery were found here.

As well as two stone circles at Trewellard, there is a medieval holy well nearby, believed to be associated with a chapel, although no trace remains of this. It was once a useful supply of horse leeches, used medicinally in humans as well as cattle.

The white sandy beach of Portheras Cove nestles between sheer cliffs at the mouth of the shallow valley below Pendeen, and it is owned by the Duchy of Cornwall. At low tide there are rocks below the sand, and sometimes grey seals haul themselves out onto the beach. In the summer it is also a good place for to see dolphins.

The path to the light. Pendeen Cliff and Lighthouse.

Until 2004, when it was cleaned up, parts of the beach were out of bounds, made unsafe by sharp fragments of the MV Alacrity, wrecked here in 1963. The British cargo ship, built in 1940 by Goole of London, was carrying a cargo of anthracite when it ran aground on the rocks and broke up.

William Borlase

Pendeen Manor House was built in 1589 of wrought granite and it came into the possession of the Borlase family in 1623. Parts of it were remodelled in 1670, but much of the building still standing is the original manor house. It has elaborately scrolled gables and an arched buttress with an ornamental parapet above, and it is of particular interest as a fine example of Cornish architecture, noted for its crenellated chimney stacks.

It was the birthplace of the Cornish prehistory scholar William Borlase, whose works included The Antiquities of Cornwall, published in 1769, and The Natural History of Cornwall, published 15 years earlier. After studying at Oxford, Borlase was ordained and became Rector of Ludgvan in 1722, obtaining in addition his native parish of St Just 10 years later. Ludgvan was an area rich in minerals and metallic fossils, and Borlase started collecting and studying these, which led in due course to a fascination with the geology, wildlife and, more particularly, the archaeology of West Penwith.

His extensive studies captured the interest of his great-great-grandson, William Copeland Borlase, who visited many of the ancient sites catalogued by his predecessor, himself supervising a number of archaeological excavations a century later.

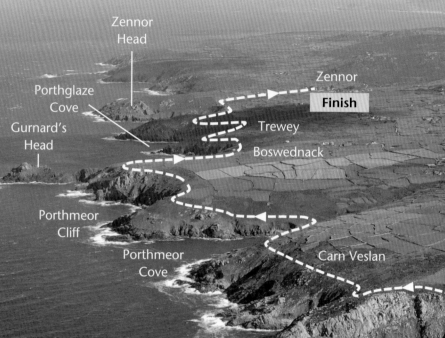

ROSEMERGY TO ZENNOR

Zennor
Head

Porthglaze
Cove

Gurnard's
Head

Zennor

Finish

Trewey

Boswednack

Porthmeor
Cliff

Porthmeor
Cove

Carn Veslan

Bosigran

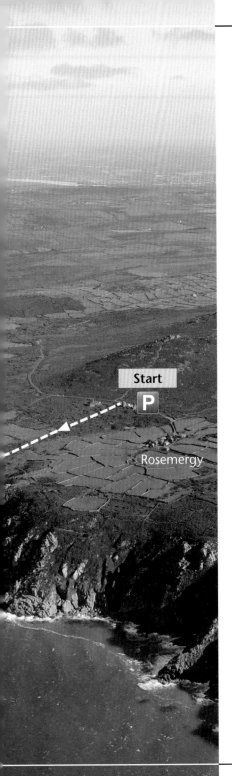

Start

Rosemergy

Walk 13 – Rosemergy to Zennor

Distance	5.75 miles (9.75km)
Estimated time	3 hours
Difficulty	● ● ● ● ○
Ascent	958ft (292m)
Map	OS Explorer Map 102
Starting point	SW 420364

Notes: A strenuous walk with a little scrambling over rocks, past spectacular granite outcrops and features from prehistoric as well as medieval times. Well-worn historic paths link the patchwork field systems with areas of remote open heathland, crossing the tumbledown stone walls by means of ancient granite stiles. Visit the mermaid in Zennor Church before taking the bus back to Rosemergy.

From the roadside car park at Rosemergy take the path beside the chimney of Carn Galver Mine and follow it downhill, past the footpath on the right, to the South West Coast Path. Turn right and climb with the Coast Path over the granite cliffs at Bosigran and around Carn Veslan and Carn Moyle Cliffs to drop into the valley above Porthmeor Cove. Cross the stream and carry on ahead and uphill to Porthmeor Cliff.

Continue on the seaward side of fields to Gurnard's Head. Detour left to visit the headland, and carry on ahead through an old mining area in the valley above Treen Cove to climb Boswednack Cliff and descend steeply into the valley above Porthglaze Cove. Cross the footbridge and continue up through another mining area on the headland above Carnelloe Long Rock, to walk above the cliffs at Carnelloe and Trewey. Heading downhill, cross a footbridge and climb steeply ahead to the

Pendour Cove where the Mermaid of Zennor lives!

Mermaid of Zennor bench end.

path at the top. Turn left to take the circuit around Zennor Head, returning to this point, or turn right to follow the footpath directly into the village at Zennor. After visiting the church, take the road up to the bus stop on the B3306.

Jane Chapel (from the Cornish word 'yein', meaning 'bleak' or 'wild') near Gurnard's Head was mentioned in the 1086 Domesday Book, and medieval pottery has been found here. It is thought that it may have originally been a pre-Conquest hermitage or a well chapel: there is a spring beside it which may once have been regarded as a holy well.

At Zennor the Norman church stands on the site of a sixth-century Celtic church. It is famous for its carved medieval bench-end depicting the Mermaid of Zennor, who is also portrayed in a bronze dial on the south side of the church tower, along with an inscription dated 1737. The

Mermaid rose from the sea and lured a local boy into her watery embrace, and he was never seen again.

One of the last native speakers of the Cornish language lived in Boswednack. Farmer John Davey (1812–1891), also a schoolmaster for some time, is said to have learned the language from his father, and could converse in his native tongue. Although there was some doubt about how much of his Cornish was genuinely native and how much was as a result of private study, he was able to recite a traditional rhyme which sceptics were unable to find in any written resource:

CORNISH	ENGLISH
A Grankan, A Grankan,	O Cranken, O Cranken!
War'n men a gawas saw vyan,	Beyond the field of the well,
Yn hans dhe Bark an Fenten,	you give but little,
Neb try lows a ven.	only three shoots by the stone.
Fordh Bensans dhe Varhas Yow,	The road between Penzance and Marazion
Hag uthek moy gwer,	is very green
Hag uthek moy cro,	and a whole lot fresher
A mag try lows a varhak,	three shoots grow for every passing horseman

Prehistoric West Penwith

The whole area of West Penwith is so rich in human history that the Heritage Gateway website, listing England's scheduled monuments and listed buildings, details no fewer than 1,270 on a search for the Zennor area alone!

While elsewhere in Britain agricultural practices have obliterated all traces of earlier field systems, in West Penwith the farming landscape has evolved around prehistoric fields, with successive generations preserving their layout so that it is still possible to see today how our ancestors lived and cultivated crops.

The very earliest settlers lived in round house settlements scattered throughout the landscape, surrounded by fields with new fields added piecemeal beyond the boundaries as required. Beyond the stone wall and banks bounding these fields was an area of common land used for grazing, as was the rough heathland on the high ground, and the trackways leading from the settlements to the grazing areas are still in use today. These Neolithic people buried their dead in communal chambers known as quoits, seen at Zennor, Sperris and Chûn, and had various ritual ceremonies attached to their ancestral cults (see Walk 11), and there are many stone circles and other monuments used for this purpose (see Walk 12).

Some time around 1500 BC there was a large-scale reorganisation of the way the landscape was divided, and the new 'Celtic fields' were smaller and more intensively cultivated, with a series of 'lynchets', or cultivation banks. The round houses of the new settlements were clustered in small hamlets and there is evidence that there was a fair division of the available land. Around Bosigran the remains of these settlements are still visible.

Later, in the Iron Age and the Romano–British period succeeding it, settlements were built within defensive enclosures on the summits of the high ground, in hillforts, and on the very tips of promontories, in cliff castles, like those at Treryn Dinas, on Gurnard's Head, and on the cliffs at Bosigran.

WALK 13

Treveal
Cliff

River
Cove

Treveal

Boscubben
Wicca

Tregerthen

Tregerthen

Wicca Cliff

Tremedda

Mussel
Point

Tregerthen
Cliff

Porthzennor
Cove

Zennor Head

Walk 14 – Zennor and Treveal

Distance	5 miles (8km)
Estimated time	2½ hours
Difficulty	● ● ● ● ○
Ascent	781ft (238m)
Map	OS Explorer Map 102
Starting point	SW 454385

Notes: A long walk through an ancient world, where the fields as well as the lanes have their origins in prehistory. It has been designated an Environmentally Sensitive Area in order to preserve this very special landscape.

In Zennor take the inland footpath between the church and the village hall and follow it through the ancient field system, past the farms at Tremedda, Tregerthen, and Wicca, to join a lane to Boscubben. Past the buildings turn left on the green lane to the farm at Treveal, staying with it as it heads to the right past the farmhouse and comes out at the cattle grid at Trevail Mill.

Turn left onto the tiny footpath to River Cove and walk through the old mining valley to the South West Coast Path. Detour ahead at the footbridge to visit the cove, but otherwise turn left along Treveal Cliff above Economy Cove, to Mussel Point and Wicca Cliff.

Cross the stream and climb Tregerthen Cliff, following the Coast Path above Porthzennor Cove to where a path leaves on the left. Take this left-hand path for a shortcut, but otherwise carry on around Zennor Head turning off the Coast Path to carry straight on ahead along the footpath, past the old coastguard cottage at Carn Cobba, to Zennor.

WALK 14

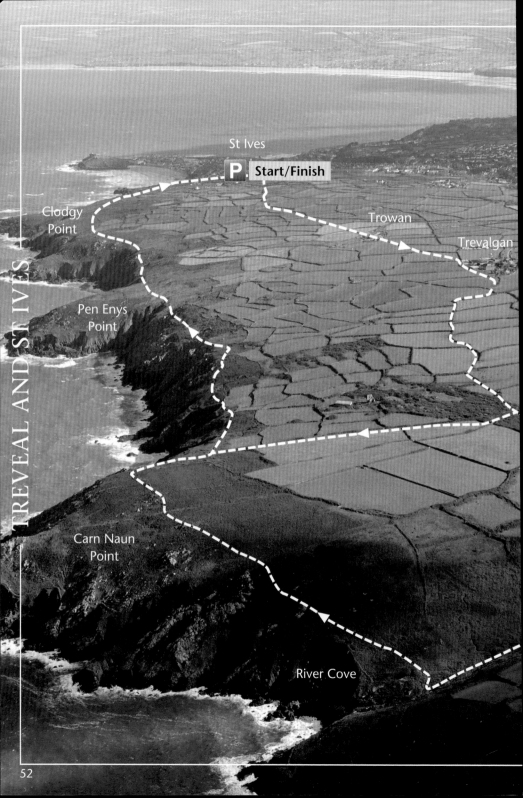

St Ives

P Start/Finish

Clodgy
Point

Trowan

Trevalgan

Pen Enys
Point

Carn Naun
Point

River Cove

TREVEAL AND ST IVES

Trevessa Farm

Trevail Mill

Walk 15 – Treveal and St Ives

Distance	6.5 miles (10.5km)
Estimated time	4 hours
Difficulty	•••••
Ascent	889ft (271m)
Map	OS Explorer Map 102
Starting point	SW 515408

Notes: On a long and strenuous route which is rocky in places and steep in others, exposed to the elements and crossing a lot of stiles, nonetheless this is a wonderful wilderness walk through a special environment. Linking it to Walk 14 gives a full day's walking with lunch in the lovely village of Zennor.

From Porthmeor Beach in St Ives, walk steeply uphill past the Tate Gallery, onto Porthmeor Hill and Alexandra Road, to turn right down Burthallan lane and then left onto the footpath towards Zennor and Treveal. Following the path through the maze of tiny fields and the hamlet of Trowan, continue to Trevalgan Farm. The path travels around the seaward edge of the farm buildings and then continues through a patchwork of a fields in a westerly direction.

After about two thirds of a mile you have the option of taking a shortcut on a path that leads out to Carn Naun Point. Otherwise continue westwards on the path as it descends to Trevail Mill. Just after the mill turn right on the tiny path to River Cove, turning right again when you join the South West Coast Path to follow it back to St Ives.

This is a long haul over difficult ground but there are plenty of distractions along the way.

WALK 15

53

River Cove.

The entire coastal strip of West Penwith is part of a Site of Special Scientific Interest, and it has a wide diversity of unusual animals, birds and plants, some of them nationally rare species. On the exposed granite cliffs wildflowers such as thrift and sea aster flourish in the crevices in the rock, while stonecrop and kidney vetch thrive on their exposed outcrops. Colonies of seabirds nest here, such as fulmar, shag and kittiwakes.

Wild flowers.

On the grassy slopes, the salt-laden air provides ideal conditions for wild carrot, sea campion and ox-eye daisy, and wild thyme and bird's-foot trefoil proliferate in the heathland above. In spring, bluebells are a splash of colour on the thin soil between the gorse and bracken, and in the summer months heather runs riot in a blaze of purple and lilac. Insects abound, too: nationally scarce butterflies such as silver-studded blue and pearl-bordered fritillary are found here, and rare beetles and snails are found beneath the undergrowth.

Peregrines and ravens wheel overhead, and these are good nesting grounds for smaller birds, too, such as stonechat, whitethroat and sedge warbler. The disused mines are the perfect habitat for bats and owls, and sometimes you can even spot a chough.

Trevassa Farm was the birthplace of Sir John Quick, a founding member of the Commonwealth of Australia. In 1851, two women found gold by the creek in the Australian settlement of Bendigo in Victoria, and among the thousands of prospectors flocking to the region from all over the world were the Quick family. John left school at 10 to become a labourer, later working on the press at the Bendigo Evening News. Teaching himself shorthand, he became a reporter and then moved to Melbourne to study law. Called to the Bar, he became a parliamentary writer instead, before being elected to Parliament as the member for Bendigo, returning to work there as a solicitor. A leading advocate of federation, he was knighted in 1901 in recognition of the role he played in forming the new Commonwealth.

West Penwith Environmentally Sensitive Area

West Penwith covers over 9000 hectares with its wild moorland, extensively farmed grasslands, sheltered valleys and coastal cliffs, and it is such a rare and precious landscape that in 1987 it was designated an Environmentally Sensitive Area.

Managed by the Rural Development Service, the Environmentally Sensitive Areas scheme was devised to protect traditional farming landscapes considered to be vulnerable. Grants are made available to participating farmers to enable them to maintain and enhance the landscape, heritage and wildlife. Central to this is the practice of using cattle to graze rough areas, as well as maintaining existing field patterns, some of which were in existence 5,000 years ago and are considered to be the world's oldest man-made structures still in continuous use (see Walk 13).

Farmers are also encouraged to rebuild Cornish hedges, restore traditional buildings, protect archaeological sites and restore habitats such as coastal heathland and maritime grassland. The scheme is voluntary, but about 90 per cent of the eligible area is currently being protected in this way.

St Ives Head

ST IVES HEAD

56

St Ives

Walk 16 – St Ives Head

Distance	2 miles (3km)
Estimated time	1 hour
Difficulty	● ○ ○ ○ ○
Ascent	95ft (29m)
Map	OS Explorer Map 102
Starting point	SW 519403

Notes: A gentle stroll around 'The Island' and on through 'Down-Along', the old fishing town of St Ives, with its granite quays and cobbled streets lined with whitewashed cottages. Pause awhile in the Tate St Ives or the Barbara Hepworth Museum, or some of the other galleries and studios which thrive in this vibrant, colourful town.

From Porthminster Beach car park, facing the beach, turn left and walk to Pedn Olva. Turn right onto the path known as The Warren, bearing right onto Pendola Walk beyond. Carry on ahead along Wharf Road, bearing right onto Back Lane and carrying on along The Wharf around the harbour, bearing right at the Sloop Inn onto Quay Street.

With the pier on your right turn left to carry on along Wheal Dream, passing the St Ives Museum to walk through the car park and on to the tiny beach at Porthgwidden. Pick up the path on the far side of the beach and walk around The Island (St Ives Head), past the coastguard lookout on the summit, with the Chapel of St Nicholas on your left. Following the path through to the car park at Porthmeor, turn right onto Porthmeor Road, turning right with it at the end of the car park and then right onto Back Road East. From Back Road West turn right at The Digey to walk above the beach.

WALK 16

57

St Ives Harbour.

Turn left after the Tate St Ives, by the cemetery, and then left again after the car park, taking Barnoon Hill to the right and carrying on past the Barbara Hepworth Museum, down Back Street. Veer left onto Lifeboat Hill and turn right and then left to pass St Ia's Parish Church. At the end of this road turn left to return to The Warren and retrace your steps to Porthminster.

Cornish Palms overlooking St Ives.

St Ives has four beaches. At low tide the harbour has a sandy shore where you can sit and watch the bustle of its quays and the cobbled streets beyond. At Porthgwidden there is a tiny sandy beach, which is a suntrap and a good place for bathing. Porthminster Beach is longer, boasting almost half a mile of golden sand, while Porthmeor is a little less sheltered and so a popular place with surfers as well as sunbathers. It is a stunning place for sunsets.

St Ives was once known as Porth Ia (Ia's Cove) after the Irish princess who sailed here in the fifth or sixth century to bring Christianity to the people of Penwith. With 777 companions she was said to have set out on a leaf which miraculously (and fortunately) became a boat, and here she joined the saints Fingar and Piala in the mission, widespread throughout Cornwall but especially on the north coast, to keep the light of Christianity burning in a land seen to be under threat from the pagan incursions of the Anglo-Saxons. She was slain on the River Hayle and buried in St Ives, where the Church of St Ia was built around over her grave, although the parish church that stands on the site today was built between 1410 and 1434. Its 80-foot tower was constructed using massive granite blocks brought here from Zennor, and its Fishermen's Aisle has clear glass windows which enabled fishermen to keep an eye on their boats in the harbour while they prayed.

On St Ives Head (also known as The Island), the little chapel is dedicated to St Nicholas, patron saint of sailors. It is not known when it was built, but there are records of its repair from as early as the fifteenth century. In the eighteenth century it was used by revenue men watching out for smugglers. In 1904 it was partly demolished by the War Office, provoking outrage in the town, but rebuilt in 1911. The floor tiles depict fishing scenes and are the work of Bernard Leach.

Art and Artists in St Ives

For well over a century artists have been drawn to West Penwith, attracted by its romantic remoteness, its ancient landscape, its traditional lifestyle, and the quality of light which allows for such richness of colour when the sun is out. By the end of the nineteenth century painters like Stanhope Forbes and Lamorna Birch had set up the Newlyn School (see Walk 1), and from the 1880s onwards there was a steady stream of artists arriving in search of a communal way of living and painting like that already established in Brittany in the art colony of Pont-Aven.

Early artists of the St Ives School included Cedric Morris, a Swansea-born painter arriving in 1925, and Christopher Wood, a Liverpool artist, who visited in 1926 and returned the following year with the abstract artist Ben Nicholson. On this visit, Wood and Nicholson stumbled upon Alfred Wallis, an unknown artist who had begun painting his seascapes in his seventies 'for company' after his wife died.

Nicholson settled in St Ives during the Second World War, as did sculptress Barbara Hepworth. Their presence started to draw other abstract artists, such as Naum Gabo, and modernism became firmly established as the town's artistic motif. Artists from other disciplines began to join as well, such as internationally renowned potter Bernard Leach, whose oriental influences derived from a childhood spent in Japan and Hong Kong, and whose studio produced many talented apprentices.

The St Ives artistic community had a Bohemian, cosmopolitan air which in itself was influenced by the light and the colourful lifestyle, and as a result the town became a centre for art and artists which still flourishes today.

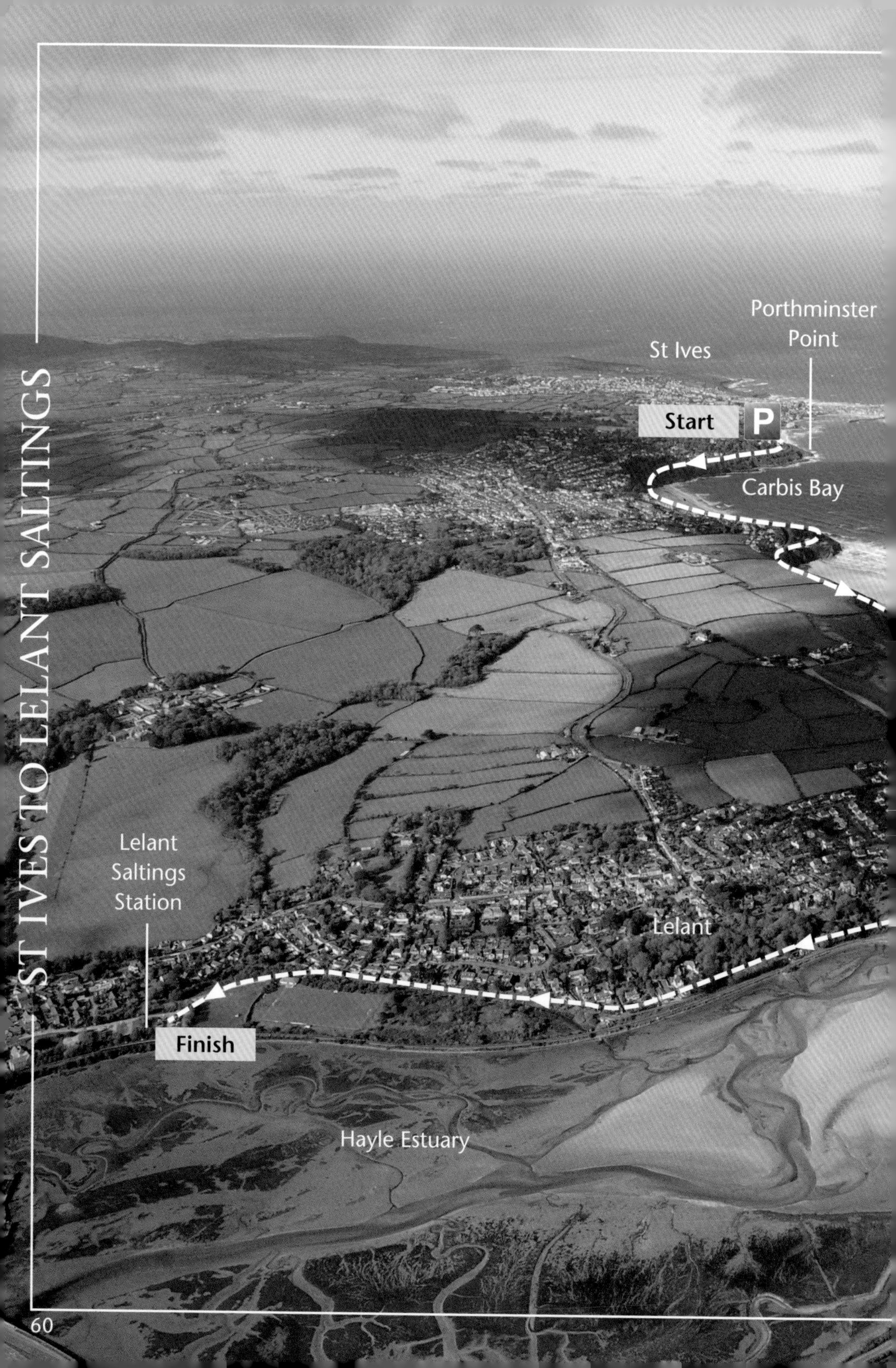

ST IVES TO LELANT SALTINGS
Porthminster
Point
St Ives
Start
P
Carbis Bay
Lelant
Saltings
Station
Lelant
Finish
Hayle Estuary

St Uny
Church

Walk 17 – St Ives to Lelant Saltings

Distance	4.5 miles (7.25km)
Estimated time	2 hours
Difficulty	● ● ● ○ ○
Ascent	301ft (92m)
Map	OS Explorer Map 102
Starting point	SW 519403

Notes: A country walk alongside the picturesque St Ives Bay Railway Line, returning by train. Although it is a long climb out of the town and up to Lelant, none of it is steep and there are spectacular views across St Ives Bay, taking in the long sandy beach at Hayle and the lighthouse on Godrevy Island. The path is exposed to sea winds, so wear warm clothing, as well as good footwear for the places where it may be muddy.

From Porthminster Beach car park follow the South West Coast Path to Porthminster Point (acquired by the National Trust in 1961), and cross the railway line on the footbridge to head up the steep path towards the huer's hut. Carry on up the tarmac path past Treloyan Manor, towards Carbis Bay. When Carbis Bay beach appears through the bushes on your left, cross the railway bridge to head down the path to the beach and then walk up towards the railway station to where the Coast Path continues on your left.

Follow the Coast Path around the headland at Carrack Gladden, heading towards Lelant. Keeping the golf course on your right, stay with the Coast Path along the Hayle Estuary to St Uny Church at Lelant.

At St Uny Church continue along the road to the T-junction, turning left and bearing left to

St Ives.

continue ahead to Green Lane and then on to The Saltings, which will lead you to Lelant Station. From here take the train back down the hill to St Ives.

In the Middle Ages Lelant was a seaport, but as sand drifted in and the estuary silted up, St Ives took over as the main port.

During the construction of the St Ives Bay Line in 1875 a number of shallow graves were discovered in the sand and shortly afterwards several stone-built cists were found, more deeply buried. Nearby was a primitive building, considered to be an early chapel, which archaeologists suggested might be the original chapel of St Uny, deserted when it was buried in sand. The burials were very similar to others found near Padstow and at Gwithian, across St Ives Bay from here,

Cornish Palms between Carbis Bay and St Ives.

which dates them to somewhere around the fourth or fifth century, during the time when Celtic saints were arriving in Cornwall in large numbers.

The first written record of Lelant was around 1150, when it was referred to as Lananta, thought to mean 'St Anta's holy place'. Although little appears to be known of St Anta, the Parish Church in neighbouring Carbis Bay is dedicated to St Anta and All Saints. Some commentators believe that it is St Anta, not St Uny or St Ia, who is connected with the chapel.

There is a tiny crumbling quay, or 'hard', at Lower Lelant, now no more than rubble. It dates from around the eighteenth century and at that time led to one of the main causeways crossing the estuary. The present, much larger, quay was built of granite by the railway company and provided access for ships at all states of the tide, with warehouses, a steam crane and a weighbridge. A ferry operated at Lelant from medieval times, and on the 1842 Tithe Map there was a 'Norwayman's Dock' in the tidal strand just south of the ferry.

There are a number of medieval crosses in the parish, including the Sea Lane Cross at the junction of Sea Lane and the main St Ives–Hayle road. These were widely used in the Middle Ages to mark the way to holy places, although sometimes they were simple waymarkers at the junctions of ancient paths. Usually these were in the form of the Celtic 'wheeled' cross, said to have been a hybrid between the Christian cross and the pagan sun motif, which were used by Celtic missionaries to attract pagan sun worshipers to the new religion.

The River Hayle is a Site of Special Scientific Interest, and the RSPB has a nature reserve at Lelant with plenty of walks. The Lelant Saltings is a substantial area of salt marsh, and it is an important place for birdwatching. In cold winters as many as 18,000 birds flock here, because this is the UK's most southwesterly estuary and it seldom freezes over. In summer look out for ospreys, and in spring and autumn you will see migrant wading birds, gulls and terns. Other frequent visitors are curlews, oystercatchers and little egrets.

While you are considering an itinerary incorporating the train journey on the St Ives Bay Line, why not join the Rail Ale Trail? This is a scheme promoted by the Devon and Cornwall Rail Partnership and supported by CAMRA, the Campaign for Real Ale, linking pubs that can be visited by train. Many of these serve locally brewed ale, and food as well, and enthusiasts can collect stamps at each which can be exchanged for Rail Ale merchandise. On the St Ives Bay Line there are five of these pubs, including one in Lelant and two in Lelant Saltings.

St Ives from Porth Kidney Sands.

Covering 630 miles from Poole to Minehead, the South West Coast Path National Trail leads you through diverse landscapes, all with their own unique story to tell. If the walks in this book have inspired you to find out more about the longest and most popular of the UK's 15 national trails, visit www.southwestcoastpath.com.

Natural England – www.naturalengland.org.uk
Natural England is the government's adviser on the natural environment and provides the majority of the funding for the maintenance of the Coast Path, which is undertaken on a day-to-day basis by Devon County Council and the National Trust. Through Environmental Stewardship Schemes, Natural England also helps farmers and other landowners to protect and enhance the countryside so that nature can thrive.

National Trust – www.nationaltrust.org.uk
The National Trust Countryside Team works seven days a week to restore and care for the characteristic wildlife of the area, as well as working with local communities to improve access and understanding of these special areas. Regular events and opportunities to get involved mean that all ages can help shape their countryside.

South West Coast Path Association – www.southwestcoastpath.org.uk
If you enjoyed these walks, why not join the South West Coast Path Association? This charity represents the users of the trail, campaigns to improve the path and raises money to help it happen. By joining you'll be one of thousands who help to make the South West Coast Path one of the world's greatest walks.

Cornwall Area of Outstanding Natural Beauty – www.cornwall-aonb.gov.uk
The Cornwall AONB makes up approximately a third of the county and is in 12 separate parts. The landscape is diverse and ever changing, cherished by those whose families have worked in it for generations and loved by those who are seeing its beauty and mystery for the first time. It is the essence of Cornwall.

Cornish Mining World Heritage Site – www.cornishmining.org.uk
With an area totalling 20,000 hectares, the Cornish Mining World Heritage Site is the largest World Heritage Site in the UK, and this status places Cornish mining heritage on a par with other international treasures such as the Pyramids of Egypt or the Great Wall of China.

SAFETY
On the beach and coast path

- Stay away from the base of the cliffs and the cliff top and ensure that children and dogs are kept under control.
- Do not climb the cliffs. Rockfalls can happen at any time.
- Beware of mudslides, especially during or after wet weather.
- Always aim to be on the beaches on a falling tide and beware of the incoming tide, especially around headlands. Be sure to check the tide tables.
- Beware of large waves in rough weather, especially on steeply shelving beaches.
- Observe all permanent and temporary warning signs; they advise on hazards and dangers. Check routes beforehand by visiting www.southwestcoastpath.com

- Be very careful on rocky foreshores which often have slippery boulders.
- Stay within your fitness level – some stretches of coast can be strenuous and/or remote.
- Make sure you have the right equipment for the conditions, such as good boots, waterproof clothing and sun screen if appropriate.
- Follow The Countryside Code.

Emergencies
In an emergency dial 999 or 112 and ask for the Coastguard, but be aware that mobile phone coverage in some areas is very limited.